This w

The Secrets for Self Growth

21 Exercises for Personal Development

Disclaimer

This book is not intended to be a substitute for medical advice or treatment. Any person with a condition requiring medical attention should consult a qualified medical practitioner or suitable therapist.

The information provided in this book is stated to be truthful and consistent, in that any liability, in terms of inattention or otherwise, by any usage or abuse of any policies, processes, or directions contained within is the solitary and utter responsibility of the recipient reader. Under no circumstances will any legal responsibility or blame be held against the publisher for any reparation, damages, or monetary loss due to the information herein, either directly or indirectly.

"Start small and keep it simple"

That's our motto for change.

Table of Contents

Introduction --vii

Instructions For Reading ---------------------------------x

Chapter 1 - It's Never Too Late------------------------1

Chapter 2 - Be a Worry-Solver------------------------5

Chapter 3 - Say Hello to Yourself--------------------9

Chapter 4 - Express Yourself Without Limit------14

Chapter 5 - Your Own Ideal VIsion-----------------17

Chapter 6 - Your Future-------------------------------21

Chapter 7 - Take Action-------------------------------24

Chapter 8 - Have a Feast, Eat, Drink & Share-----26

Chapter 9 - Ask Your Higher Self for Advice-----29

Chapter 10 - Being Grateful--------------------------34

Chapter 11 - Get Your Bad Habits On Stage-------37

Chapter 12 - Trade Your Bad Habits----------------43

Chapter 13 - Explore Nature-------------------------46

Chapter 14 - The Art Of Giving----------------------48

Chapter 15 - The Art of Receiving--------------------52

Chapter 16 - Don't Waste Your Talents, Live Your Passion---55

Chapter 17 - Reading Self Growth Books Will
Change Your Life--60

Chapter 18 - Be a Millionaire For One Day--------65

Chapter 19 - Dear--68

Chapter 20 - Collaborate------------------------------ 70

Chapter 21 - Stretching Your Comfort Zone-------75

Personal Journal--81

INTRODUCTION

We want to thank and congratulate you for purchasing The Secrets for Self-Growth, 21 Exercises for Personal Development are awaiting. No, it's not another patronizing, 'this-is-how-you-should-do-it' guidebook. We will provide something different. There are tons of self-help books out there, but reading alone won't do the trick. It's about doing and using what you've learned. That is why we created a self-growth workbook. To put you in the lead.

A preview of the clear and challenging exercises that will help develop your life overall:

- Identifying your biggest regrets in life
- Solving or accepting your current problems
- Trading a good habit for a bad one
- Becoming a millionaire for one day
- Discover your higher self

"An ounce of action is worth a ton of theory." **Ralph Waldo Emerson**

We don't have infinite wisdom that will solve all your problems. What we can do is provide you with reliable exercises for self-growth, inspired by the greatest self-growth books and mentors from ancient China to the finest thinkers of modern time. Some of these exercises are common sense while others may seem a little out there. For those exercises, we want to encourage you to get through your initial skepticism and test yourself. It's in the unknown where remarkable insights can be found.

Do you want to be right or do you want to be happy?

There are different ideas, different possibilities, and different answers. The world is evolving. Old ideas become new and new ideas become old. As people we never know it all. Yes, you might be wrong. We might be wrong. Do all the exercises and reflect on them: what did you learn? Being a lifelong learner and listening to advice from others is one of the greatest skills you can gain in this life.

Learning and trying something new doesn't

mean you have failed. It means you can challenge your comfort zone and sharpen your thinking. Don't be afraid of this. It's never as worrisome as it seems. We welcome you to give our exercise a try and cross the border of change. So, where are you looking for? To know the answer, you first need to determine the question. Why do you read this introduction, go to seminars and watch yet another self-help video on YouTube? What the question is? It's up to you. That question will guide you through these exercises. And the answer? That's a secret, waiting to be revealed...

INSTRUCTIONS FOR READING

You will have the best experience doing one exercise at the time. The exercises are in order so it is possible to go from one exercise to the next conveniently. If you want an even better understanding of the book, you could first read it all the way through without stopping to do the exercises. Lastly, you can use the Personal Journal at the end of this workbook for taking notes during the exercises. Good luck and enjoy!

'Life Starts Today'

There is never a better moment for change than right now.

True Potential Project

1. It's Never Too Late

Exercise: What is something you regret in your life? Either accept it or take action!

Whatever your age, we all have things in life that we regret. Adventures that never took place, missed opportunities in love, businesses that never came to life… Time goes on, and life continues without pause. New opportunities and more responsibilities. In random moments, the past can haunt us. Regrets about what could have been. The more you think about it, the bigger the sadness becomes and the more difficult it is to release yourself from the tenacious and forceful grasp of regret.

"Forget regret, or life is yours to miss."
Jonathan Larson (1960-1996), American Composer &
Playwright

Regret Is an Appalling Waste of Energy

The approach is to accept or change the situation. As for regrets, a similar solution applies. Whatever you regret in life, obsessing over it and blaming yourself for not taking the opportunity won't solve anything. Use your energy and your time to make conscious, peaceful and fearless decisions. It's not too late to still chase your "left behind" desires or make peace with your situation as it is. In Exercise 2 we will talk more in depth about coping with worries.

Exercise: The first exercise in this workbook is identifying your biggest regret in life. Think about this regret and make a conscious decision. Is there still a possibility to go for this opportunity, maybe in a different way? If so, and you still feel the deep urge to go for it, by all means, take action *today*! Don't steal yourself from the life you're capable of living. Remember this quote by the late John Barrymore, a famous actor in the early Hollywood years, "A man is not old until regrets take the place of dreams."

Some regrets involve opportunities that no longer exist. For these regrets there is but one possibility to find peace: accept the past as it is.

This is a process that can take time. It's

important to start this accepting proce ㅗ
possible. Remember, there is never a be
change than right now.

Release the Burden

If you eventually accept a lost opportunity of the past a substantial psychological burden will be lifted. Don't let your mind trick you into thinking your life is over because you lost one opportunity. It's just not true. Find peace with your past and tap into your inner wisdom to find new ideas and answers that will lead you to new opportunities.

You could also consciously decide for yourself that your regret is part of your past and you no longer seek to chase that opportunity. You live a different life now with new opportunities. Kindly accept your past as it is and move on.

Tip: If you have a hard time getting over regrets, it could be very helpful to write about this missed opportunity and let these feelings out. Otherwise, you'll keep thinking about the past and the *what ifs*. The longer you lurk with regrets the more thickening the cloud of negativity, pessimism, and melancholy becomes.

you confront these feelings, it will be easier to deal with your regrets over time by either accepting them or finding the strength to go for them once again.

"It is never too late to be what you might have been."

Mary Ann Evans, "George Eliot" (1819 - 1880), British novelist

2. BE A WORRY-SOLVER

Exercise: Make a list of worries in your life, and then take action by solving one immediately

The opposite of self-growth is being imprisoned by negativity and worries. When you let them, worries can occupy your mind 24/7. They will be the rulers of your empire and you will be a mere slave. While there are concerns in life, our worries typically are about situations yet to come or worry about the past. You do not know what the future holds and you cannot change your past, so why punish yourself? The famous Mark Twain quote is a guideline to live by.

"I've had a lot of worries in my life, most of which never happened."

Samuel Langhorne Clemens, "Mark Twain", American author (1835 - 1910)

It's Not All About Positivity

Is it all about positivity? No, that's way too easy. Horrible things can and do happen in life. There are plenty of real concerns to consider. But, we can deal with these concerns in two ways. We can either accept them or make a change. Worrying has never solved *any* problem. However, thinking about solutions and consciously acting does. Now, focus on your worries for a moment.

Yes, they're but mere thoughts. Nothing more and nothing less.

We can't predict the future and we can't alter the past. We realize that this is *way* easier said than done. Yet, you owe it to yourself to at least practice this way of thinking and living. Start with seeing your worries for what they are: thoughts. Creations from the fearful part of your mind.

Accept or Change

We will say it again, either accept your concerns or change your situation. You could worry about your financial situation, relationship, health, weight or any other concern, but it won't go away by obsessing over it!

Accept the flaws of your partner or sit down

for a heart to heart talk. Accept your body for what it is or exercise and stay away from fast food. Accept that in your current situation you can't make time for your artistic dreams or spend at least 45 minutes a day on your writing. Don't worry—just accept or change the situation.

Exercise: Make a list of worries in your life and take action by solving one immediately. Get in the habit of confronting and solving concerns promptly. In this exercise, you will make extensive lists of all your current worries. Think about all the areas in your life and what, specifically, makes you anxious.

Step two is to look at the list. If you see these worries on paper, are they still *real* worries? Maybe you can scrape off a couple worries already.

The last step is picking one worry and either solving the problem immediately or starting the process of acceptance. Try to get into the habit of either accepting or solving your concerns directly when they arrive. As we said earlier, this is way easier said than done, but it is more than worthy to be heroic and escape your prison of worries.

Tip: The book *The Way of the Peaceful Warrior* by Dan Millman is a fascinating and inspiring story about how to live in the "here and now" instead of allowing worries to control your life. The audiobook version of the book is done by the author himself. Also, the book has been made into a movie of the same name.

3. Say Hello to Yourself

Exercise: Connect With Your Inner Wisdom

The third exercise in this book will be one that works as fuel for other exercises. Connecting with your inner wisdom is vital if you want to improve yourself. It's the connection to the wise, strong, endlessly loving and always understanding part of ourselves that can guide us through dark and difficult times. This higher self will support you to achieve your greatest goals. We all have this voice of inner wisdom. No matter what your current life situation is, it can fight for you. When you use your inner strengths, self-growth will be your default setting.

Note: In this book, we will use both "higher self" and "inner wisdom" as an equal term.

"When you operate from the Higher Self, you feel centered and abundant— in fact, overflowing. When you experience this abundance, your fears automatically disappear."

Susan Jeffers author of *Feel the Fear and Do It Anyway*

Different Parts

It's essential to recognize that we could operate from different parts of ourselves. For instance, when you eat chips on a couch while watching a reality show out of procrastination, you act from a different personal part of yourself than when you give a killer presentation at work. Fear, excitement, and other emotions, together with thoughts and external situations, lead to different behaviors from different parts of us. Our higher self is often overlooked. Between our worries and other toxic thoughts, this part hardly gets a chance to be your own wise counselor.

Fortunately, this inner wisdom remains no matter what. You can connect to it wherever and whenever you want to. If you haven't ever done so, or haven't for a very long time, it will take more effort. No matter what, though, your own personal counselor is ready to serve you.

Self-talk & Silence

Through self-talk and silence, you can connect with your inner wisdom. You can hear your higher self when you pay close attention or ask direct questions. For religious people, this might feel like a spiritual experience. If you aren't religious, connecting with your higher self is just as important and possible for you. See it as your inner infinite wisdom. In times of stress, tough decisions and suffering, this inner wisdom gives a sense of comfort, calmness, peace, and encouragement. Let it guide you toward the creativity that leads to new solutions, astounding ideas and great artistic work.

Perhaps the concept of self-talk sounds strange, mystical or even comes across as utter nonsense to you. Whatever the case may be, we invite you to try this exercise with an open mind. It's extremely important to bond with yourself in order to improve yourself. Be your own best friend and trust the process.

The most helpful approach to doing this is by connecting with your inner wisdom.

You will find an incredible wisdom inside of yourself that can lead to a sense of calm. Although worries, pain, and fear may not dissolve entirely or even quickly, it will help you find a solution to problems—or perhaps even the power to accept difficult situations in life for what they are.

Exercise: Connect at least once a week for one month with your inner wisdom. Determine a part of life where you have worries. Recognize and accept it, then go to a peaceful place in your house or out in nature. Give yourself some time to slow your thoughts down. Then, ask this question: I worry about _____ situation; can you give me advice on how to deal with it?

Do a session of at least 15 minutes. Use the first 5 minutes to slow down your thoughts. Meditation is suggested here. Then ask your question and start a self-talk. If you don't get anywhere the first time, don't worry! Try again next week. Sometimes it takes time to connect with your higher self, especially when you're not used to doing so.

Tip: If self-talk and inner wisdom sounds odd to you, keep it light and fun while you try this exercise. Nobody will judge you, so don't worry about that. Just give it a try and maybe you will surprise yourself.

4. EXPRESS YOURSELF WITHOUT LIMIT

Exercise: Dance and sing like no one's watching

Sometimes there are so many overwhelming thoughts and worries bottled up inside of us, it seems impossible to gain clarity. Demanding jobs, busy family life and social expectations magnify our to-do-lists. And they just keep growing. It's too much: you want to let go. Scream! Go crazy? That's normal. It's energy. It's fine to let it out. Every so often, it's important to break free—either to celebrate life or to deal with its hardships. When we give in, the cloud of worries and toxic thoughts can melt away. You'll feel more alive— more joyful—if you allow yourself time to *move*. Rise above the limits that other people and societal expectations throw at you. Dance, sing and

14

celebrate life!

"There are shortcuts to happiness, and dancing is one of them."

Vicki Baum, Austrian author (1866 - 1960)

No One's Watching

Concerning the above quote, we'd like to add singing to the shortcuts to happiness list. Both dancing and singing help to get you out of your head. They cut through all the negativity. When let go at home, whether you sing or dance, don't look to achieve anything. Just do it for *you*.

Like dancing and singing, sports can also help to get you out of your own head. Biking, running or even walking for at least 20 minutes a day, or setting aside time for a quick workout, can make all the difference. Just remember, you don't *have* to win anything. Don't push yourself too far. Just take some time for yourself and let go.

For this exercise, there are no expectations. Sing out of tune or dance like a wiggling grizzly bear—it doesn't matter! You have *no* audience and there are no judges analyzing your every move.

After this dance and singing session, we think you will find a renewed energy, a healthy loosening of tight, sore muscles and a sense of happiness that's uniquely yours.

Exercise:-Pick out one evening and schedule a dancing and singing night just for you or invite a group of friends. For the first time, we suggest you do it on your own so there are absolutely no expectations and you don't have to worry about what anyone is thinking. Do it for at least 20 minutes. Pick out some songs, close those curtains, shut the door, turn up the volume... and have FUN!

Tip: You have to take life serious at certain times. Raising your children, juggling your finances and job expectations, etc., may call for more responsible behavior. That's a good thing! Just don't forget the other side; don't ignore the necessity to give yourself a break. This is a perfect exercise to get you out of the habit of taking life — and yourself — too seriously *all* the time. Don't forget to enjoy life; it will make living a much more joyful experience.

5. Your Own Ideal Vision

Exercise: What's your ideal vision for your own life? Dare to dream big and put it on paper!

Self-growth begins with knowing what you want. What's your direction in life? We sometimes feel the pressure to make *something* out of our lives—and that's normal. However, without a clear direction, stress comes in and it's hard to ignore. What do I want from my brief time on this Earth?

Our lives never stay the same permanently. Peaks and valleys, remember? While fluctuation in life is normal, you don't want to catch yourself in a downward spiral for decades, years, or even months. Take matters into your own hands and determine your course.

"We are haunted by an ideal life, and it is because we have within us the beginning and the possibility of it."

Phillips Brooks, American Preacher (1835-1893)

Express yourself without limit

A compelling vision is a driving force for all of our goals. There should be no hesitations and no limitations when you write this vision. It's just on paper for now, but who knows? Dreams can come true, right? This is similar to the previous exercise: Express yourself without limit. Instead of singing and dancing, now it's about writing all your deepest desires and biggest hopes. Being a millionaire, building an AIDS-hospital in Africa, traveling through the southern parts of Asia, having a family or driving a Lamborghini—it's up to you!

What we want to create in this exercise is a compelling vision that is *truly* yours and one that is more or less realistically achievable. Do you dream of being a millionaire but at the moment you're dead broke? That's okay; we *still* think the dream is absolutely achievable. Just read the stories of self-made millionaires. One guru in the 'becoming rich niche' and also a multimillionaire himself, T. Harv Eker, began as a broke young man coming who moved back in with his parents three times before becoming successful.

Endless Possibilities

There are endless possibilities as long as you have a plan, the determination, and the persistence to take consistent action toward your vision. In the next two exercises, we will break your ideal vision up into achievable goals for the foreseeable future. You will make a game plan and take instant action.

For now, there is no time limit. Dream big and write your compelling vision.

Think about the purpose behind your big vision. WHY do you want to have a family? WHY do you want to become a millionaire? WHY do you want to build a hospital in third-world countries? Your purpose is the driving force behind your ideal vision. It stands side by side with your values in life.

Exercise: Make a compelling, ideal vision for your life and write it down. You could also add photos (from your ideal house, bank account, family picture, audience, etc.) to conceptualize your ideal vision. When you're ready, try to visualize yourself in your ideal life. How would you feel? How would you look? How would you behave?

Tip: Set up a weekly or monthly event in your calendar to check your ideal vision. Your ideal vision could change overtime. In the next exercise, we'll dive deeper into being flexible enough to alter your goals and vision whenever life, or a change in what you're passionate about, calls for it.

6. YOUR FUTURE

Exercise: Think about your goals for the foreseeable future

From the larger-than-life vision in the previous exercise, we'll now dive deeper into the nearby future. In the sixth exercise of this *21 Exercises* workbook, you will set your goals for the foreseeable future. Think about the short-term: one month, three months, or up to a year away. This way, your goals will become real and attainable. With short-term goals, there's also an undeniable call to action. For the moment, we'll just focus on breaking down your ideal vision into short-term goals.

"If you don't know where you are going, you'll end up someplace else."
Yogi Berra, Famous Baseball Player (1925 - 2015)

Making a Life Box

To break down your ideal vision and to gain an overview of your life, we suggest making a Life Box. Think about all the important areas of your life and put them in a different box. Different areas could be Family, Career, Health & Fitness, Friendships, Religion, Self-growth, Contribution, Relationship / Dating Life, Finances, Traveling or Hobbies. You will most likely have somewhere between seven to eleven different boxes.

The next step is prioritizing these different areas and ranking them in order of importance. These boxes are an honest, clear and ordered overview of your life. Maybe you even want to reconsider your ideal vision after making one— and that's okay, too!

Not Written In Stone

Your ideal vision is not written in stone. It can fluctuate and is organic like all things in life. Things can occur in life that will impact your ideal vision. We can't control everything that's going on in our lives. It's paradoxical. You need to be very persistent and consistent when you want to achieve your goals in life, yet you also need to allow flexibility so that you can alter your life goals when circumstances change or your ever-changing interests demand a new course and new goals.

You can *always* decide what *you* want in life.

Don't let your dreams and desires be beaten down by everyday life and worrisome thoughts. Whenever a situation calls for a radical change in your life plans, rely on the purpose and values behind your ideal vision. They can guide you to a new path in life.

Exercise: Come up with at least one goal or a maximum of three goals you'd like to achieve in the foreseeable future. This could be for next month, three months, or even up to one year. It's recommended that you make it as short-term as possible. Making short-term goals will give you a higher urgency to take action.

Tip: If you are into productivity and goal-setting then the *12Week Year* system might be perfect for you. It's a system designed for achieving goals in the nearby future. This system is all worked out in the book *12 Week Year* by Brian Moran and is also available as an audiobook.

7. Take Action

Exercise: Come up with at least 10 actions for every goal you have established in Exercise 6. And... Take action on one of these steps immediately!

We will pick up where we left off in the previous exercise. You've set your goals for the foreseeable future. Now it's time to take action. Put things in motion. It's the art of self-growth, realizing what you want, setting a plan and taking conscious and consistent action. The small actions you take today will lead you one step closer to your ideal vision in life.

"The distance between your dreams and reality is called action."

Anonymous

The above quote says everything you need to know. The goals you have set in the previous chapter of the *21 Exercises* workbook will only come alive when you take action. You could have all the knowledge, all the plans, but if you don't take action, it's useless. Go ahead. Read the above quote again. Don't forget it!

Exercise: Come up with at least seven actions you could take to achieve one or more goals you have set in the previous Exercise. Take action on one of these steps immediately. For example, your goal is to set up a blog with three articles, two YouTube videos and to gain an e-mail list of at least 50 followers. Your first action could be writing up an article, building the website or taking a creative writing course.

Tip: When you're struggling with procrastination, this book is a great read: *The Power of Self-Discipline* by Brian Tracy. It's helpful for when you're feeling less than motivated. For artists, we advise *The War of Art* by Steven Pressfield. It's an inspirational and (warning!) *very* demanding book that aims to help inspire you to get your artistic work done.

8. HAVE A FEAST, EAT, DRINK & SHARE!

Exercise: Organize a dinner for the people you love

The best moments in your life might be the time spent with the people you love. When we truly connect as people, magic happens. The first time you hold hands with your crush, the moment your daughter spoke her first words or a good friend providing you comfort after a big loss. These are times we feel understood and we feel that we belong to something bigger than ourselves.

"You won't know how much you'll miss someone until they're gone. Go give them a big hug while you have the chance."

Kevin Focke, Belgian Author

A Fine Night

Who do you love in your life, is it your close family? Close friends? Teammates? Whoever they are, being together with them is a great source of satisfaction for you. If you think about our mortality, about life being short, why waste another day? Grab the chance to celebrate life with your loved ones. A fine night with food, good wine and beer, and fantastic stories will bound you together. It's the kind of night where you can give the people you love a big hug—while you still have the chance.

To make it extra special, ask everyone to dress in a certain style. Men in suits and women in cocktail dresses. Or mix it up! Go for a special theme! How about the '50s, superhero night, or James Bond?

Exercise: Organize a get-together for the people you love. Make a nice dinner at home or go to a restaurant. Be the planner. Make it happen—even if you're on a budget. You can still organize a great dinner. Invite everyone to bring their own side or drinks and enjoy!

Tip: The world famous cook Jamie Oliver has a website with great dinner party's recipes. Check out   his   website   for   inspiration: http://www.jamieoliver.com/recipes/category/occa sion/dinner-party/

9. Ask Your Higher Self for Advice

Exercise: Identify a burning question for yourself and do a guided visualization to find the answer

In Exercise 3 we introduced the higher self. The inner wisdom centered inside each of us. In this exercise, we will ask our inner wisdom for advice once again. We all have worries or burning questions we want advice for. Maybe you're thinking about quitting your job, worrying about how to raise get through to your eldest son or what to do with your spare time. All of these questions have a lot of different options. Should I do this? Or should I do that? We get conflicting and confusing information about ourselves and other people. The choices and worries seem only to become more complicated. What is it that you actually want?

"At the center of your being you have the answer —you know who you are and you know what you want."

Laozi, Ancient Chinese Philosopher

A Meditation Technique

An in-depth and effective technique to find your own answers is through guided visualization. In this meditation technique a guided voice, either through an audio CD or a YouTube video, leads you through a meditation. It is preferred to do this meditation with your eyes closed in a comfortable position, either sitting or lying down. First, you slow down your thoughts and get yourself to relax by focusing on your breathing or repeating a mantra.

After your thoughts have slowed down, the guiding voice will give you further instructions for visualization. These instructions will lead you to seek advice from your inner wisdom concerning a burning question or ongoing worry. A guided visualization is also perfect for creative inspiration.

Dreamlike

By concentrating on visualization you will both see and hear advice as if you are in a dream. It could be a stunning and powerful experience that will help you to identify what it is you have to do in life. Or, at the very least, it will give you some great new insights about your problems.

If you're new to meditations, you could start by first listening to recorded meditations *without* meditating. This way, you'll know what to expect!

30 minutes

In the tip section of this exercise, we've chosen 30 minutes of guided visualization. It may seem long, but embrace this time for yourself. Because of the guided voice, you won't have to do it all on your own. 30 Minutes will be enough time to both relax and build a strong connection with your inner wisdom. We've also added two guided meditations (with an introduction to visualization) for beginners in the tip section as well.

There are various other guided meditations that could prove helpful. These meditations rarely focus so much on visualization but more on positive and supporting affirmations. Meditation for weight loss, overcoming anxiety and dealing with insecurity are some examples.

Exercise: Identify a burning question or big worry. With this question in mind, do a guided visualization to seek advice from your inner wisdom. For example, "what do I need in my life right now?" What happens when you ask that question? What do you see? After the guided visualization, take a moment to drink water and reflect on what you saw and heard during your visualization. You could write your experience down if you want to!

Tip: These are 3 helpful YouTube meditation videos to help get you started. If you search on YouTube, you will find lots of guided meditations.

A 30-minute Guided Visualization Meditation:

https://www.youtube.com/watch?v=rw-FtDxOyPY&index=14&list=LL20t-pbWR9vlHDK89Cc5X3w

A 5-minute Guided Visualization Meditation:
https://www.youtube.com/watch?v=i50ZAs7v9es

A 5-minute Guided Meditation for Beginners:

https://www.youtube.com/watch?v=LDu4-dyA7DE

10. BEING GRATEFUL

Exercise: In the next 3 days write at least 100 things in life you're thankful for.

What is life without gratitude other than the passing of time? Without gratitude, the miracles of daily life elude us. Our friendships and family, our careers, our own, unique talents, the grandeur of nature, the beauty of art and the excitement of sports — it can all surpass us. Through constant worry and toxic thoughts, we forget how much we have. Think of how unique you are, how amazing even the challenges you face can be, and how much love you can receive from those closest to you. With a focus on gratitude, day-to-day life turns into a miracle itself, where we can find joy in even the small moments.

"Gratitude can transform common days into Thanksgivings, turn routine jobs into joy and change ordinary opportunities into blessings."
William Arthur Ward, American Author (1921 - 1994)

For this exercise, we will shine the spotlight on everything we're grateful for. It could be as significant as your children or friendships or as small as your colleague's smile every day when you come into work. You could be thankful for specific moments, such as that great dinner five years ago with school friends near the old university, or the day you got a nice compliment from a total stranger. Think about moments you're grateful for over the next three days and write them down in your notebook. After those three days, look at the list and keep it safe. As you think about the list, we anticipate some smiles, some emotions creeping up. That's gratitude. It can transform your life.

Exercise: In the next 3 days write at least 100 things in life you're thankful for. You could use your notebook that serves as a personal journal for this workbook. Make sure you keep the list for review. Every time you feel negativity or just a little bit down, take a look at the list. There's still plenty enough to feel thankful for.

Tip: The 5-Minute Journal is a beautifully designed workbook that enables you to think about your grateful moments each day and measure the results. It's available on this website: www.intelligentchange.com. You could also use your own notebook and make it a habit of writing three things you're thankful for every night before you go to sleep.

11. GET YOUR BAD HABITS ON STAGE

Exercise: Find the root of the problem when it comes to your bad habits

Bad habits can sabotage your self-growth. They can endanger your health, finances, close relationships and other major areas of your life. Habits like fast food, watching TV or shopping are not necessarily *bad*. Most of the time they give instant gratification and can even be a well-deserved reward after a day of hard work. When we consistently engage in these habits over a long period, however, they become our comfort zone. If we're not conscious enough, these habits can become addictions.

"Correcting bad habits cannot be done by forbidding or punishment."

Robert Baden-Powell (1859-1941), Lieutenant in the British Army

Addictions

If bad habits have the power to become addictions, they have the power to self-destruct our lives. Think about it. You love watching TV every now and then. It's your habit to watch TV or Netflix every other night for at least one hour. Not that much, right? It's still a habit, nevertheless, because it's an action you repeat over time. So watching TV or videos online becomes a part of your comfort zone. Your comfort zone is full with habits and that provide you with feelings of safety. What do you do whenever you face challenges in your life? Exactly. You retreat to your comfort zone. Make sure it's the kind of zone you want to be in.

For example, you have debts and you know by proper budgeting or working extra hours you can solve your bad financial situation. To do so takes courage. It's far easier to watch TV and ignore these issues instead. Your bad financial situation doesn't disappear and the worse it gets, the safer you feel in your comfort zone. It provides you with an escape, so you run the risk of multiplying these comfort zone actions. Instead of watching TV every other day for one hour, what if it becomes *every* day and more?

Thick Clouds

Another possibility is that your habits could numb you so much that you don't see the challenges and sticking points in your life anymore. Your habits are the thick clouds in your life through which you cannot properly glimpse reality anymore.

Look at your own life and be brutally honest with yourself. Do you recognize any bad habits in your own life? Habits that already, or have the power to, push you away from self-growth and your deserved happiness in life? If that's the case, I invite you to read further.

We all have bad habits; it only takes courage to admit that you have them. The multimillionaire whose smoking 10 cigarettes per day, the professional athlete with a sex addiction, and the mother of three kids who spends hours a day on virtual gaming are just a few examples. Maybe yours aren't as extreme; however, habits have the power to grow. Whatever you continue will enhance. It's the law of nature, either in an upward or downward direction. In this exercise of the 21 Exercises workbook, we will shine the light on our bad habits so we know why we're doing them.

Again, it's a no-brainer. You have to reward

yourself from time to time. Fast Food, drinking alcohol, binge watching series every so often isn't bad! What we are talking about in this exercise is when it becomes an unhealthy habit.

Exercise: Find the root of the problem when it comes to your bad habits. This is a 4-step exercise:

1. Identify your bad habits and rank them, with number 1 being the bad habit that has the most negative influence in your life.
2. Shine the spotlight on your bad habits. Ask yourself, "What do I try to avoid by nurturing this bad habit?" In other words, what is the real problem?
3. Think about it for a while and write the answer in your notebook. A self-talk for answering this question is highly recommended.
4. Plan to deal with the root of your bad habit immediately or set a date to do so. You won't solve an underlying problem like a lack of self-confidence instantly. However, by making a commitment to deal with the problem and act on it there is an opportunity for real and lasting change.

Here's an example of answers to the above questions. We will only examine the bad habit with the most negative influence.

Paul, a 32-year-old journalist, has identified three bad habits. His number one bad habit is:

Excessive working out

- He asks himself the question through self-talk in a quiet room in his apartment.
- The answer he came up with is this: "I am doing excessive workouts to go to the gym and avoid too much time with my girlfriend. Actually, my relationship hasn't been good for a while now. It's easier leave than to confront the tough situation with my partner."
- Paul makes a commitment to have an honest heart to heart talk with his partner the same evening.

Tip: Besides communication problems, another underlying problem of bad habits is usually a lack of self-esteem or a lack of purpose in your life. You're insecure about your body, so by eating fast food you'll feel happy for a short time and can forget about your insecurities. Or you feel a lack of purpose in your life and buy compulsively so you experience immediate gratification which replaces your lack of purpose.

A great book for improving your self-esteem is The Six-Pillars of Self-Esteem by Nathaniel Branden.

For finding your purpose in life we advise to look at Exercise 9 once again and to read exercise 16 & 17 with special attention. Personal coaching, reading inspiring books, enrolling in self growth programs and attending certain seminars are also useful when you want to determine your purpose in life. Whatever you do, some heavy soul searching is sometimes required to find your path in life. Even if you know what you want in life, the outcome is never certain. That is critical to remember. Sometimes you need to simply choose an option and give it your all.

12. Trade Your Bad Habits

Exercise: Exchange a bad habit for a good habit for a period of one week.

In the previous exercise, we examined the underlying problems of our bad habits and how to identify and attempt to solve them. Now it's time to *change* our bad habits. Or, even better: trading our bad habits for good ones. Gear up for a week of excellence. Show your bad habits the door and allow some new guests to arrive.

"We are what we repeatedly do. Excellence, then, is not an act, but a habit."
Aristotle, Ancient Greek philosopher

Welcome to the exchange market of habits. We have already identified all of our bad habits, so in this exercise we recommend choosing one habit you would like to change for a week. This could be the bad habit that has the most negative influence in your life, but you may also opt for another one.

What you will gain in this exercise is the experience of being in control of *changing* your actions in a positive and improving way. A bad habit out, a good habit in. Trade your complaining for one week of optimism and compliments, your chips and chocolate for apples and carrots or your procrastination for one week of determined and consistent action.

Exercise: Exchange a bad habit for a good habit for a period of one week. Start small and keep it simple—that's our motto for change. Once your time is up, we think you'll notice a difference. Be honest with yourself. Was this helpful? If so, try it out for another week and then another. If you struggle or give into bad habits while you attempt this exercise, don't be discouraged. Try again!

Usually, it takes 21 to 60 days to establish a new habit. Some habits are more easily established than others. It can be very difficult to change habits, but it can undoubtedly improve your life in ways you can't imagine. When you want success in life, remember the famous quote of Aristotle: "We are what we repeatedly do. Excellence, then, is not an act, but a habit."

Tip 1: If you want to track your new habit, the internet era provides you with multiple tools to do so. We recommend habit tracker apps you can download on your smartphone. These apps, mostly FREE, not only track your habits but also send you reminders. Good apps are *Habitbull* & *Loop Habit Tracker*.

Tip 2: Excellent further reading for understanding and changing habits: *The Power of Habit* by Charles Duhigg

13. EXPLORE NATURE

Exercise: Go into nature for a nice, long walk or a bicycle tour

There are a lot of real problems and challenges we have to face, and most of the time we can't ignore them. In this *21 Exercises* workbook, we encourage you to face these problems and challenges in your life. Small problems have the power to grow into crises if we don't tackle them early on. In this exercise, we will focus on relaxation. Relaxation is as important as problem-solving. Go outside and enjoy the beauty of nature. Rest, relax, recharge.

"Open your eyes and see the beauty."
Unknown

Being Comfortable

For this exercise, go on your own. Find a park, a trail, etc., and go for a nice, long walk or a bike ride. You don't have to do anything. No self-talk, no meditation. Just be there. If weather permits, bring food and a book and treat yourself to a picnic. It's up to you.

Earlier, we talked about being your own best friend. That involves being comfortable on your own. If you can love and respect yourself, you can love and respect others. Make a great day out of this excursion and enjoy the calmness and simplicity of nature. After you've completed this exercise on your own, you could try it out with friends and family.

Exercise: Go into nature for a nice long walk or a bicycle tour. Enjoy being on your own. Don't rush yourself by making plans about what to do. Leave your worries at home and relax.

Tip: Leave your smartphone at home. Disconnect. This way, you won't be disturbed by Facebook posts, Instagram selfies or group apps.

14. THE ART OF GIVING

Exercise: Give something away for free

We share this planet. We share the same insecurities and the same dreams. Above it all, we share our love and the need to connect with each other. Without sharing, there is but cold indifference. To share, we need to both receive and give. We give money to a charity. We receive a nice compliment. Good, loving energy needs to flow from one to another. Be open and be willing to give and receive. Someone who receives love honestly and thankfully will be significantly more likely to give love in return.

"Be generous with your blessings. A kind gesture can reach a wound that only compassion can heal."

Steve Maraboli, Behavioral scientist & author

It's Not a Numbers Game

In this exercise of the *21 Exercises* workbook, we will work on giving. Honest giving with an open heart is one of the most beautiful actions in life. It can be as simple as sharing some kind words with a person who needs to hear them. Lightening the burden of someone in pain can be done by just listening to their story and empathizing. It doesn't require much effort to make the world a better place. It only takes a little.

You can build schools in Africa or dedicate your life to better education for disadvantaged people. It's very noble to live a life to serve others. For most of us, however, this isn't the life we have chosen. We are driven by different passions and different responsibilities. It's inspiring to know any act of kindness could make a magnificent difference in not only the life of others, but in the world.

Thomas

We all know a story similar to this. Thomas, a 26-year-old university graduate, wanders through the streets on a cool summer night in Chicago. He is a talented guy, at least that's what everyone keeps telling him. He's not so sure about it, though. For months now, he seems to have lost his purpose in life. No girlfriend, no consistent income to pay off his college loan debts, and no particular hope for a better future. His artistic dreams are long gone and his chosen job field is too competitive. A question is haunting him. Is he throwing away his life already? These were supposed to be the big years. The best years. Exciting romances, adventurous holidays and a sensation of independence.

Yet, here he is strolling down the streets of downtown Chicago—and something amazing happens. If it wasn't for Thomas running into his old high school teacher, Mr. Reynolds, things might have stayed the same. They had a long walk that night. Mr. Reynolds listened to Thomas's worries. For the first time in months, Thomas let someone in. He shared his doubts and his long forgotten dreams. Eventually, their ways parted. Mr. Reynolds put a hand on Thomas's shoulder and said, "You're going to be okay, kid."

Three years later Mr. Reynolds received an invitation for Thomas's wedding in Hawaii. There was a special note included, which said, "You were right. Thank you. Sincerely, a delightful father and groom to be."

Exercise: Give away something without expecting something in return. It's up to you what to do. The only thing that is essential is giving with an open heart and full attention. Here are some examples:

- Offer free coaching or mentoring in your field of specialty to someone young and inexperienced
- Volunteer at a homeless shelter
- Organize a (small) charity and raise money for a charity of your choice
- Clean out your wardrobe and give your leftover clothes away to a charity

Tip: "Giving" doesn't have to involve charity. It could also concern giving *honest* compliments or surprising the people you love with a getaway.

15. The Art of Receiving

Exercise: Receive without hesitation and enjoy your gifts

The introduction in Exercise 14 covers most everything on the value of both giving and receiving. It may seem strange to make an entire exercise about *receiving,* isn't it one of the easiest things to do? Sadly enough, most people would not agree. How often do you treat yourself without feeling sorry for doing it? How often do you receive a compliment without lessening your own actions that *deserve* the compliment? Not that often, right? We thought so. The following exercise is perfect for you. Do you think you already receive plenty? Well, it's okay to receive a little more!

"Giving feels fantastic and for there to be a Giver, there must be a Receiver, so allowing yourself to receive is an act of love."

Rebecca O' Dwyer, Irish Author

Receiving can be beautiful. As we read in Thomas's story, it can also be life-changing. What if he hadn't received the kind words and advice from his former teacher? If you lock yourself into your own little world of worries, it's hardly possible to receive wholeheartedly. To receive, you need to open yourself up. You must *accept*. Receive compliments, take advice, or help. It's an act of love.

Exercise: Try to be conscious for one week about receiving without hesitation and with an open heart. Whenever someone wants to help you or gives you a compliment—embrace it. To emphasize this feeling, plan one action for this week where you can receive, relax and enjoy. A massage is perfect for this.

Tip: Look at the "Being Grateful" list you made in Exercise 10. It's plenty, isn't it? Be thankful for what you have and rest assured you will receive many more things to be thankful for in your life!

16. Don't Waste Your Talents, Live Your Passion

Exercise: Spend at least 30 minutes a day this week on something you absolutely love

The responsibilities of everyday life frequently interfere with our most enchanting dreams and our *real* talents. With a thousand things to do, it's normal to wonder where the time has gone. One day you are 21, and then suddenly—in the blink of an eye—you are in your mid-thirties. Sometimes it feels impossible to cope with time. Where are the dreams that shot to life when you were 12-years-old and life seemed easy with no restrictions?

> "There is no passion to be found playing small - in settling for a life that is less than the one you are capable of living."
> Nelson Mandela (1918-2013)

Tap Into Your Greatest Strengths

Your unique talents and callings will never be erased. Maybe you feel the calling to blow off the dust from your old dreams and thrive in ways you would have never imagined. Being a better parent, become a novelist, being a contributor to the poor and undeveloped in this world, starting your own business or finally having that loving relationship you have longed for. And the good thing is? Living your true passion can start as soon as today. This is not a cheesy marketing line. This is the truth.

Whenever we tap into our greatest strengths and our biggest dreams, something amazing happens. A new flow of life-energy is released through you and goes out into the world. For those of you who have a true passion but are stuck waiting for the right moment to take action or, even worse, think your dreams are unrealistic, there is but one piece of advice: start today!

But...

We hear you thinking. My job, my family, my character, my debts, my age, my study, my, my, my. Don't you believe you were put on this Earth to do the absolute most with your time and unique talents? Chase that calling and fight for what you want. Think about these questions and be honest about your answers. Remember that it's not too late; the best time to start is always right now.

Adversity

If you've taken the first step already, you know how good it feels to be on the path of following your dreams, challenging your talents and living with passion. However, while it's nice at first, adversity can set in. After a couple of days, or weeks, or months. That's the first price you have to pay when you are on this freeing path. Still, we urge you to fight your limiting beliefs and negative thoughts—and don't forget to ignore the negativity from other people. It will be there, too.

This is why we encourage you to take small but consistent steps. Make it a habit of spending a little bit of time per day on something you're passionate about. At first, it could be as small as thirty minutes. This way, you will become more used to this new activity of doing something you're passionate about. You will build up a defense that will benefit you whenever adversity sets in.

Dreams can always change. That's part of life. It's not a fundamental "must" to achieve your dreams, but we think it *is* a must to be on the journey *toward* your dreams. Try. That is self-growth. Commit to something you're passionate about—it's part of this journey.

Exercise: We invite you to make this a week where you tap into your greatest strengths and biggest dreams. This exercise is to spend at least 30 minutes a day for one week on something you absolutely love. If you are already doing so, try to give yourself even *more* time per week on learning your particular craft. Whether you do it for seven straight days or decide to skip the weekend, that's up to you. Here are five examples for this exercise:

Examples:

- If you want to become a better parent, read a book on parenting every day and plan quality time with your children at least three times a week

- If you want to become a novelist, you could start with structuring the outlines for your future novel for 30 minutes a day

- If you want to build your own business, research your niche and come up with at least 10 actions you could take to kick-start your business

- If you want a loving relationship, read books on dating advice or join dating apps and websites

- If you are passionate about being more self-confident and want to shed some weight, commit to working out and drinking more water instead of sodas and alcohol for a week

Tip: An outstanding book on tapping into your great strength is *The Big Leap* by Gay Hendricks. In this book, he explains in detail how to live in your "zone of genius." The book is also available as an audiobook.

17. READING SELF-GROWTH BOOKS WILL CHANGE YOUR LIFE

Exercise: Read or listen to (audio) books on self-growth

Reading books can be life-changing. Literally! We can't stress this enough. One of the hardest struggles in life is the fight between your consciousness and your worrisome and complaining thoughts. This negativity never seems to diminish. But, if we read books on self-growth and fill our minds with positive and self-improving thoughts, we can challenge our limiting beliefs, worries, and personal negativity. We're connecting with our inner wisdom to create the consciousness we need to be happy and have success in life. Go ahead. Read. Try it yourself and reap the fruits of knowledge.

"Whenever you read a good book, somewhere in the world a door opens to allow in more light."
Vera Nazarian, Russian author

The Key to Success

For thousands and thousands of people all over the world, including the most successful people in our era, reading books on self-growth is the key to lasting success and a more fulfilled and happy life. In the tips section of this exercise, we will give you some great book recommendations on self-growth. Most of these books are also available as audio books.

If you're not a reader, this is an ideal possibility to consume these books. Reading fiction is advised because this will help your literacy and imagination. In this exercise, however, we'll solely focus on books concerning self-growth.

No matter what, give this exercise a try. For the more experienced readers, we have an extensive list added to this exercise. Pick a book you haven't read yet and dive into yet another world of amazing self-growth.

Exercise: Read a book on self-growth, or listen to an audiobook, and try to finish it within two months. Or, for more avid readers, you could try to read a book a week for one month. That will mean reading one hour every day. For people preferring audiobooks, if you want to get the information faster, you could always speed up the audio. We recommend taking notes during reading. If the books have work sections, complete the exercises that are written in the book to get the most out of the experience.

Tip: We have compiled list of books worth your time. If you have any questions on further reading, please contact us at our 21 Exercises Facebook page (www.facebook.com/21Exercises/).

Book Recommendations

Self-growth (General)
The Big Leap by Gay Hendricks

The Six Pillars of Self-Esteem by Nathaniel Branden

The Slide Edge by Jeff Olson

Think and Grow Rich by Napoleon Hills

Outwitting the Devil by Napoleon Hills

The Subtle Art of I Don't Give a F*ck, by Mark Manson

Unleash the Power Within by Anthony Robbins

Feel the Fear And Do It Anyway by Susan Jeffers

The 4-Hour Workweek by Tim Ferris

The Art of War by Sunzi

The Power of Habit by Charles Duhigg

Inspiring and Spiritual

The Way of the Peaceful Warrior by Dan Millman

The Alchemist by Paulo Coelho

The Power of Now by Eckhart Tolle

Man's Search for Meaning by Victor Frankl

Ego is the Enemy by Ryan Holliday

Finance

The Richest Man in Babylon by George Samuel Clason

Secrets of the Millionaire Mind by Harv Eker

The Cashflow Quadrant by Robert Kiyosaki

Rich Dad Poor Dad by Robert Kiyosaki

Productivity

No Excuses! The Power of Self-Discipline by Brian Tracey

The 12 Week Year by Brian P. Morgan

The War of Art, by Steven Pressfield

Overcoming Addiction

The Disease to Please by Harriet B. Braiker

The Gambling Addiction Recovery Workbook, by C.W. v. Straaten

No More Mr. Nice Guy Robert A. Glover*

*Also self-growth (general).

18. BE A MILLIONAIRE FOR ONE DAY

Exercise: Treat yourself big time

For most of us, the infinite possibilities of wealth seem to be impossible to achieve. Well, what if it's not? Think about what wealth actually means to you. What is wealth beyond the materialism such as buying that Ferrari, spending weeks of vacation in Bermuda or a VIP treatment in a prestigious nightclub? We think wealth stands for the freedom to do whatever you want, whenever you want, wherever you want. An abundance of possibilities. This means we can all be a millionaire for at least one day.

"Abundance is about being rich, with or without money."

Suze Orman, Personal Finance Expert

Habits of a Millionaire

Think about the following questions. If you were a millionaire for one day, what would you do differently? How would you feel? These answers are the guidelines for your "Millionaire Day."

You could buy extravagant clothes, treat yourself to a long massage or go out for a fancy night on the town complete with dining and dancing with no limits, no restrictions. Or, being a millionaire could mean something entirely different to you. Maybe it's a normal day except you do not worry about anything and instead of staying in you go out for a nice meal. It can be subtle and low-key.

It's up to you, as long as you genuinely feel and behave like a millionaire for one day.

Now you have the money to do something extraordinary. Try to dig deep into what being a millionaire means to you. What if you knew with absolute certainty that you could find the means to conquer your painful financial situation in the near future? It is possible: thousands of others have paved the way for you. Escape "reality" for one day and settle back in the world of hopes and dreams.

Exercise: Be a millionaire for one day. First, think about these two questions: If you were a millionaire for one day, what would you differently? And how would you feel? Next, schedule your Millionaire's day in your calendar and when the day arrives, thoroughly enjoy it. Reflect on how this day was different from your usual days. What can you learn from it? Notice this and try to incorporate this abundant feeling in your everyday life.

Tip: Read a book on personal finance. These recommended books have the potential to be life-changing not only in the area of your finances but in your life as a whole. Worries about money can be devastating, so take a chance and commit to controlling your financial situation for good. Recommendations: *The Richest Man in Babylon* by George Samuel Clason, *Rich Dad Poor Dad* by Robert Kiyosaki and *The Secrets of The Millionaire Mind* by T. Harv Eker. These books are also available as audio books.

19. DEAR...

Exercise: Write a thank you and encouragement letter to yourself

We've almost finished all the exercises in this workbook. Now, it's time to write a letter to yourself. Some of you may think this is silly or childish, so we ask you to turn off that cynical part of your brain for a short time. Maybe this exercise will benefit you or maybe it won't, but take a little risk with your time and find it out.

No Quote

No quote in this exercise. Space is open, so it's up to you. Your own letter or your own poem, even your own quote will do. Pat yourself on the back and encourage yourself to keep going. When adversity strikes, trust yourself. Believe in *you* when everyone and everything seems to be against you. Focus on the enormous power that rests inside of you. Rise, conquer and march on.

Create your own message that will encourage you to keep going even when all seems lost.

Exercise: There are no guidelines for writing this personal letter. It could be a short message or an extensive letter. Try to recognize your achievements in life and write a compelling encouragement that could guide you through darker days.

Tip: In the introduction we asked you if you wanted to be right or wanted to be happy. We want to emphasize this again. Never feel too good to learn. It could turn out that advice or exercises are just not your cup of tea *after* you've tried—and that's okay! At least you tried and gained experience. Who knows? One day, some of the advice or exercises you learned here might surprise you.

20. Collaborate

Exercise: Create a mastermind group with like-minded people

A mastermind group is a concept that is discussed in the self-development classic *Think and Grow Rich* by Napeoleon Hills. A group of like-minded people support and inspire each other and share their knowledge, all with the goal to grow both professionally and spiritually. Whenever you want to achieve something in life, it is always easier with the support and inspiration from others who will build you up while telling you the truth in an encouraging way. A mastermind could be created with friends, members of an online forum, a Facebook group or people you meet at social gatherings. As long as you share the same interest or have the same mindset toward self-growth, a mastermind can become a success.

"No two minds ever come together without, thereby, creating a third, invisible, intangible force which may be likened to a third mind."

Napoleon Hills (1883 – 1970), American author of *Think and Grow Rich*

Starting a Mastermind

How do you start a mastermind group? First, think about the topic for your mastermind group. Will it focus on business, career, health and fitness, self-development, relationships, lifestyle, or something else? If you have defined this you can think about what kind of people could get involved. If you have as much as two people (we advise a maximum group of four to six) you can already start your mastermind group. The members should have an intention to grow, give genuine advice, be trustworthy and practice positivity.

If you want to start a mastermind group with bloggers, you could do some research and find bloggers that have more or less of the same level of followers. Join their Facebook groups and post a message in which you propose your mastermind group idea or send your proposal to these bloggers in a personal message. In this message, explain what you specifically want out of the mastermind group.

The First Meeting

When you have enough members, set the date for your first mastermind group meeting. You could do this online through Skype or Google Hangouts if distance is an issue. In this initial meeting, get to know each other a little better and set the rules for the coming meetings. Clarify that a mastermind is formal, structured and focused on growth for all the participants. People need to be brutally honest to each other, yet always maintain a level of encouragement and inspiration. To create this atmosphere, a mastermind group should be a place of trust.

It's very important to make the meetings consistent, this way you will all benefit.

It's not just a nice gathering. A mastermind group is productive. If you do it professionally, it will welcome your unbiased opinions, stress accountability, increase inspiration and, of course, you'll grow together.

Exercise: Create a mastermind group with like-minded people. Think about the topic for your mastermind group and invite suitable people to join. Set up an initial meeting, create the rules together and meet on a regular basis.

Examples for mastermind group rules:

- Meet once a week or twice a month for one hour per meeting.

- Start each meeting with positive experiences that each member of the group achieved that week (for about 10-15 minutes).

- Every week one person is in the hot seat, so he or she could discuss their struggles in the past week, the development of their projects or share knowledge and inspire others (40-45 minutes).

- The person of last week's hot seat is the moderator for the next mastermind group, so he or she keeps track of time, encourages everyone to take part in the exercise and takes the lead over the conversation when needed.

- Make the mastermind group a priority and put it on your calendar.

- Members can't miss two consecutive group

meetings.

- What happens in the mastermind group stays in the mastermind group!

21. STRETCHING YOUR COMFORT ZONE

Exercise: Act, despite fear, for one week straight.

Your comfort zone is one of the most attractive places to live in. It is warm, cozy and safe. Your long forgotten dreams and unfulfilled desires are stretched beyond the borders of your comfort zone. Read any self-help book to know about the importance of getting out of your comfort zone. Although we agree with this, we would like you to try it out for yourself. There's only one way to do this and that's by taking action in the last exercise of this *21 Exercises* workbook. You will have a week of stretching your comfort zone. A week of absolute growth: acting despite any fear.

"It is not necessary to try to get rid of fear in order to succeed."
T. Harv Eker, author and motivational speaker

Acting In Spite Of Fear

To feel fear is normal. To succeed in life and to achieve your goals, you must act *despite* fear. It's very difficult to get rid of fear altogether and that isn't the goal of this exercise. The goal is, rather, to be aware of fear. Once you identify it, you can consciously decide whether you let fear control your actions and behavior.

Remember, you are not your fear. It's just the mind talking.

With consciousness, you can support your own desired decisions. It may take a while before you've mastered this and that is fine. Just take small steps to go in the right direction. In the tip section, we share a great book about conquering your fear.

For this exercise, we go back to the concept of your life box. The overview of all the important areas of your life. Most likely, you have fears concerning all of these areas.

The Level of Fear

The level of fear you feel for certain actions is different. For example, at your job you want to be a little more social with colleagues. A task you could do is making sure you approach at least one colleague a day and chat for a while. Yet, if you want to talk with your boss about your current job because you want more responsibility, the option of working remotely from home, etc., that specific action might be a lot more scary and out of your comfort zone.

In this last exercise, you confront a different area of your life every day, starting off with the most important area of your life, as determined in your Life Box. Then, go to the next most important area and so on. For every area, define two things you are afraid of, one that involves an action that is way out of your comfort zone and one that is *not* so far out of your comfort zone. For the most fearful action, put an exact date and time in your calendar to act on it. As for the other action, take action today.

At the end of the week, you will have at least stretched your comfort zone seven times. Also, you've set seven specific actions to enhance your comfort zone even further. These are life-changing shifts.

Taking Responsibility

Needless to say, and this goes for all the exercises in the workbook, it is up to you to take responsibility and do the actions you've put on your calendar. In this workbook, some exercises might not resonate with you. However, we encourage you to go for the exercises that are challenging your comfort zone. What do you have to lose? Maybe you will even surprise yourself and your own skepticism. If not, you at least defined your own standards, values, and tastes!

Exercise: Determine your life box for every area in your life. Define for each area one action that is just a little out of your comfort zone and one action that is *way* out of your comfort zone. Act on the first today and plan for the second. If you want to do the weekends off, that's fine! Just do the other actions next week.

Tip: An excellent book for challenging your own fear and stretching your comfort zone is *Feel the Fear and Do It Anyway by* Susan Jeffers. In this book, she explains why fear exists and how to overcome it. At the end of each chapter, there are insightful exercises to challenge your comfort zone and to act in spite of fear.

Thank you!

Before we go to the final thoughts, we want to thank and congratulate you for making it all the way to the end. We sincerely hope that some of these exercises helped your progress of self-growth. Start small and keep it simple. To stay in touch you can like our 21 Exercises Facebook page where we give regular updates and useful tips about topics related to self-growth. We respond on every single Facebook message, so if you have any further questions or want to share your thoughts about this book, please be our guest! Lastly, if you could be so kind to leave an honest Amazon review to spread the message of this book, we would highly appreciate it. Now it's time for our final thoughts.

Final Thoughts

We have reached the end of this book. No more advice. No more quotes. No more exercises. Our job is done. Now, it's up to you. Did you find where you were looking for?

Pursue your dreams or stay where you are. In the end, is there a difference? You get to decide.

If you went to the doctor for a routine check-up and, horrifically, the doctor said you were going to die, not in a year, not in six months, not in a week, but that very same night, how would you look back at your life? What would people say about you? What was your contribution to this planet and humanity?

Your life: What did you make of it?

Most likely, you're not going to die tonight. So the answers to all these questions are not definite yet. You have time. What will you do with it?

PERSONAL JOURNAL

Personal Journal

PERSONAL JOURNAL

PERSONAL JOURNAL

PERSONAL JOURNAL

PERSONAL JOURNAL

PERSONAL JOURNAL

PERSONAL JOURNAL

About *21 Exercises*

We are a group of four people dedicated to self-growth. In our own mastermind group, we have a commitment to never stop learning and we believe in sharing the lessons we've learned. This book details our own personal lessons and journeys. We'd love to hear *your* ideas, tips and questions. Let us know at our 21 Exercises Facebook page (www.facebook.com/21Exercises/).

93128022R00057

Made in the USA
Lexington, KY
12 July 2018